HWA Poetry Showcase XII

Edited by

MAXWELL I. GOLD

First published by Horror Writers Association 2025

Copyright © 2025 by Horror Writers Association

All rights reserved. No part of this publication may be reproduced, stored or transmitted in any form or by any means, electronic, mechanical, photocopying, recording, scanning, or otherwise without written permission from the publisher. It is illegal to copy this book, post it to a website, or distribute it by any other means without permission.

First edition

ISBN: 979-8-9934485-0-3

Contents

Note from the Showcase Editor, Maxwell Gold	v
I Wore a Girl by R.J. Joseph	1
Every Drop by Greg Jones	3
Benaeath My Narrow Iron Bed by K.A. Schultz	4
White Nightmare by Angela Sylvaine	6
Stone Silence by Cassondra Windwalker	8
False Prophet by Tiffany Michelle Brown	10
The sky is bleeding tonight by Daniela E.	12
Amyloid Lamentations by JG Faherty	14
Tenebrae Semper Sunt by Gabrielle Faust	16
I Don't Like That We Have Two Heartbeats by Caitlin Marceau	18
Iphigenia, After by Ann K Schwader	20
Gone 11 Days Before Anyone Could Be Bothered to Look in...	21
Eugenics in the Modern Era by Colleen Anderson	23
Not That Kind of Compost by Viggy Parr Hampton	25
Boneless by Graham Masterton	27
Pine Box by Paul Lonardo	28
Pretty Little Thing by Julia Jackson	29
This Is What We Do to Gender Inspectors, So Don't Get Any...	31
Ennui by Jean-Marie Romana	33
The Bile Tooth by Stephanie M. Wytovich	34
I Write a Rite of Pyrite by Katherine Quevedo	35
I Will Come For You by Paul Duff	37
The Bundles by Annie Neugebauer	39
Night Stalker by Pauline Yates	41
Playthings by Melissa Burkley	42

Three Final Girls Take the Border Bridge (Orient, Maine) by...	44
Transit Zombies by Jamal Hodge	46
Lone Star Blues by Robert Perez	47
immersion learning by Carlie St. George	49
Menopause Monsters by Louise Worthington	50
Raft Bodies by Erik Hofstatter	52
The Water Horse by Manny Blacksher	53
It's Not a Game to the Dead by Juleigh Howard-Hobson	54
Odessa Black by David Ghilardi	55
The Ghoulish Abyss by Sara Tantlinger	56
Glass Alphabet by Ivy Grimes	58
Fruit Fly Summer by Jamie Lackey Stefko	60
What a Mother and Daughter Know about Breathing by Crystal...	62
The Planet's Darkside by Deborah L. Davitt	64
Summer's Gone by Azzurra Nox	66
Flesh Tears by Daniel Kipps	68
Peonies by Eric Machan Howd	69
Portrait of a Slaughterhouse by Grace R. Reynolds	70
Night Shift at the Asylum by Spencer Keene	71
The Memory of Her Demise by Richard Groller	73
me, mary and todd by Jan-Andrew Henderson	75
Sleep ("haamujen uni") by Ron Riekki	77
Necromantic by Christine N. Rifkin	79
The Wasp in the Wine by Vishesh Abeyratne	81
The Drowning of the Virgin Queen by Andrew Robertson	83
Author Bios	85

Note from the Showcase Editor, Maxwell Gold

It is indeed bittersweet that this will be the last *Showcase* I have the distinct honor to edit. I'd like to thank the judges; Jonathan Maberry, Cynthia Pelayo, Bryan Thao Worra, and Jewelle Gomez for lending their time and expertise to review the almost 200 submissions we received.

I'd also like to thank Dan V. Sauer for his exquisite cover art design that carries on the artful tradition of the *Showcase* brand. Lastly, thank you to the HWA Publications Committee for their constant advocacy in pushing new and exciting opportunities for the horror writing community.

Dark poetry is thriving, and to see the amount of new poets who submitted to this year's showcase gives me much joy for the future of speculative and dark poetry.

In the words of the great Allen Ginsberg, "Poetry is not an expression of the party line. It's that time of night, lying in bed, thinking what you really think, making the private world public, that's what the poet does. images, controls the culture. I don't do anything with my life except romanticize and decay with indecision."

It is that time, and there's only more to romanticize, make beautiful, and create in a world that truly, deeply desires the touch of the poet. I'm pleased to present the 2025 *HWA Poetry Showcase Volume XII*.

I Wore a Girl by R.J. Joseph

I wore a girl once just to see
if her skin fit better than mine.
It did not.
And I got mistaken for
another girl who was neither of us.
I wore a girl another time
just to see if I could only take
the parts I wanted different,
taking great care to hide the seams
to restraighten the hair
and keep the skin from decaying
into blackness.
It did not matter.
I was again mistaken for
another girl who was neither
me, the first, or the other.
I wore different girls
different times and my
big feelings never squeezed into
theirs, my kinky hair never squished
into submission.
And they always called me by
another name, never my own.
Not one from the girls I wore.

Did they know?
Could they tell I was trying
to be something, anything,
other than what I am?
They could not have known
because all they saw, no matter
who I was wearing was the same
chasm of Blackness that looked just like
all the other things they did not
care about—they did not even care
about the girls I wore.

Every Drop by Greg Jones

Every wound, gushing, soaking
A requiem of millions, choking

Every throat, pumping, pouring
Echo sighs of our adoring

Every lapping, frantic tongue
Gorges deep, this well been sprung

Every tremor, as you're bleeding
Mirror the spasms of our feeding

Every open, seeping vein
Flesh it pales, as you drain

Every carcass, tapped and chilling
A testament to mouths they're filling

Every harvest, every crop
Every human, every drop

Benaeath My Narrow Iron Bed by K.A. Schultz

Between the inhale and the exhale
I hold my haggard breath
To *listen, listen, listen...*
For what – or who – might lie
Beneath my narrow iron bed
In stealthy, hungered, still repose
Waiting, waiting for me
Wanting me to at last let go
So that the crack in this subsistence
Is split a littler wider
To permit a momentary breaching
Of my waking terror's crumbling plane
For a crippled and a slithering reaching
Of a spindling, crooked kind of arm
To out and up and slowly around
Ascend the sides of my soiled mattress
Grab at the edges of my soured bedding
Creep past the sharp-edged, little links
Which painfully my arms affix
Braceleted, infected wrists
One each, to each opposing post
Of this narrow and rusted iron bed

BENAEATH MY NARROW IRON BED BY K.A. SCHULTZ

Where I reside in enforced unrest
In an unlit room of a rotting house
In which another – I think – resides
Whose face I have as yet to behold

From behind that hand-stitched, bloodied mask
He wears whene'er he comes to "see" me…

And so, I hold my haggard breath
To let the fissure widen
In deepest hope that what – or who – might lie
Beneath my narrow, iron bed
Will be the one to slither 'round
And be the one to get me first

White Nightmare by Angela Sylvaine

Smiles welcome to Port Kaituma's
shack-lined mild west main street,
boomtown for gold mines smelling
of sulfur, staining rivers mercury orange
Beneath the buzz and click of cicadas
children whisper of evil ghosts, Jumbees,
like the slaveowner Dutchman of Guyana

Rutted roads twist past stilted houses
washing lines hung, chickens milling
Scrawled script reads "Welcome to Jonestown,"
The People's Temple, blighted tropical flower

Jones' infected tongue promised paradise,
lianas vines hacked, ironwood cleared
for his dictator's pavilion and throne as
palms wove walls of devout dorms
The Red Brigade patrolled, guns and crossbows
aimed, ordered by the father to keep in the faithful
Death Tapes tell of White Nights, rehearsed
consumption of poison and propaganda

Far away Concerned Relatives cried, so
Ryan's delegation came with cameras

Jones demanded revolutionary suicide, fed
followers from tubs of cyanide and grape

Bodies blanketed the clear-cut swatch
approaching a thousand dead by poison or bullet
A hole in Jones' head wisped smoke and soul,
a new Jumbee to rival the cruel Dutchman
Torrential rains and gusting winds avenged,
returned huts to loam as pariana grass cloaked
metal skeletons, now nests for hornets and hives

A marble gravestone sews the scar that
spiderwebs through veins of gold
We witness and pledge never again but
madmen still preach and promise, washing brains,
mixing drinks for the next people's temple

Stone Silence by Cassondra Windwalker

cloud-dappled my eyes and blistered my feet,
I keep to the path the river bids me,
though he goes east and I go west,
until I go north and he goes south

aspen leaves rain gold around me,
so I add my silver to the coins
that heap the forest floor,
peeling away my skin in moon-gilt scales
I set afloat on the whispering wind

and oh! what it whispers:
a mockingbird, it mimics
the murmur of my every bone
as it crumbles into dust,
and joins in raucous dirge
the crow who sings me home, home, home

home, where mushrooms sprout
from bare footprints sunk deep in muddy loam,
where unlidded eyes gaze
through the monocles of fiddlehead ferns,
where fetid flowers crawl and creep
with unjointed fingers

along rain-scoured grooves that spell
the name of a girl I once knew

up and down the riverbanks I go,
my tongue in one hand
and my teeth in the other,
my jaw unhinged
to hold the back door to the universe

but my voice –
   my voice was buried without me.

False Prophet by Tiffany Michelle Brown

You prophesized my destruction,
Envisioned my lips painted in blood,
My heart heaving as it fought to stay beating.

You fed the universe honeydew promises
That reeked of my extinction and your exaltation.

You grew confident as your plans took shape,
Your shadow reflecting a cunning jackal
Rather than a tired man seeking recognition.

You thought it would be easy,
To lure me in with your
Whisky smokestack breath,
Fingers practiced for pleasure,
False flattery that you wrapped around my exposed shoulders
Like a butter-warm blanket fresh out of the dryer.

You thought your love would make me malleable,
A soft plaything,
A googly-eyed girl who was finally saved and savored.

You didn't know that the knowledge among women is arcane,
And limitless,

And carries its own prophecies.

You were surprised when I bit back,
Coaxing forward the pain you sought to elicit from me.

You expected to bring about death,
Not to dance with it,
Especially with such a practiced lead.

Your vision wasn't nuanced,
Didn't embrace the paradox of supple curves
And a steady hand.

But you see it now,
The truth reflected in my eyes,
How you were always meant to fall,
While me and my sisters
Continue to rise.

The sky is bleeding tonight by Daniela E.

The sky is bleeding tonight,
it stopped crying recently, but now it bleeds and it does it so well.
Go up, go up, carry me around sadness,
carry me from pain and let me melt.
I cut a piece of meat and as I bring it to my lips a drop falls bouncing on the plate,
maybe it's too rare.
The taste of the meat is so bitter, it almost disgusts me,
but I gorge on more and I will do so until I'm full.
Go up, go up, carry me around sadness,
carry me from pain and let me drown.
As my teeth tear the pieces of meat, the taste seems more and more rancid.
Perhaps it's the taste of death,
perhaps it's the taste of putrefaction,
of flesh that rots without the evil that grips it anymore.
It disgusts me, just as the existence of the being that carried this heart in its chest
disgusted me.
Go up, go up, carry me around sadness…
The sky is bleeding tonight,
it stopped crying recently, but now it bleeds and it does it so well.
And I chew it,
I chew it with the taste of contempt.
And I satisfy myself,

like a soul finding its place in the world.
Go up, go up, carry me around sadness,
carry me from pain and let me make fun of it.

Amyloid Lamentations by JG Faherty

Failure of the brain
An organ's end of life
The organ, the one that makes me who I am
But no longer
Cells deteriorate; too fast, the doctors say
Regeneration no longer happens
The battle is lost
Deoxygenation, plaque, cellular rigidity
Neurologist-speak for you're screwed
Who you are disappears
Memories, chunks of time, pieces of me
Words come out wrong, emotions boil over
Muscles spasm and lock
Shame becomes a constant companion
Guilt never far behind
Those thoughts and feelings never disappear
Goddammit, how does it know
Which cells to kill
So that life becomes unlivable
Failure of the brain
It makes me argue, makes me forget
Angry, sad, screaming, crying
Me, them, her; her most of all
Why does only the good, the now, get stolen

Who are these people
Where is my family, where is my wife
Who took them from me
Wait, I know you, you were young like me
What happened
Who did this to you
Go away! You're not her. Not real.
Who is that in the mirror
Not me
Who am I

Tenebrae Semper Sunt by Gabrielle Faust

Flayed layers of existence,
Stretched and tanned and bleached dermis,
Subcutaneous incisions,
Nerve endings pulled out
One at a time,
Like a missed stitch,
A broken thread,
All painted the absence of color.
That neuropathy of white noise,
Propagated to purify the evil,
The voices that chitter
The indecencies denied,
Always denied…

Step into the falsehoods of the light
The warped and craven
Once shied from,
Starving little vampires,
Now growing brazen and bold
In their fermented, festering bitterness,
Malignant blight
Driving the light away
Until the tanned bleached hide
Greens and grays,

Spores taking root
To eat away and gather dirt
Upon the graves,
Freshly dug…

You feel it, don't you?
That old familiar familial darkness
Lingering within,
The truth of your self
Your worst fear,
Knowing the darkness
Is always here.

I Don't Like That We Have Two Heartbeats by Caitlin Marceau

I don't like that we have two heartbeats.
I don't like that when we hold each other,
when my naked skin is pressed against yours,
that I can feel where I end and you begin.
The space between our flesh,
the millimeters that keep all of me
from falling into all of you,
the imperceivable distance between
the atoms that force our souls apart,
all feel like miles between us.

I don't like that when my fingers come away bloody,
bits of gore still trapped beneath my nails,
that you're the only one screaming.
I want your voice to echo in my throat,
for the pain to take root in your nerves
and blossom behind my eyes.
So I shout and cry and beg until you're silent.

I don't like that I have to tear you open,
spreading you wide to bring us together.
It's a sacred act, but it feels unholy,

as I demolish the church that was you
to build the cathedral that is us.
Quivering and vulnerable,
your body is a refuge I find salvation in.
Your bones welcome me,
each break and snap a prayer of what we'll be.

I don't like that I can't taste your words on my tongue
or see the world through your eyes,
even as I wear your sinew as my own.

I pull you closer,
using my arms to use your arms to hold me tight,
and wait for us to finish coming together.

I don't like that we have two heartbeats.
But if I'm patient, soon we'll only have one.

Iphigenia, After by Ann K Schwader

You killed me for a wind the gods withheld
to keep your fleet from Troy. Or so men said,
so often & so loud you felt compelled
to spill my blood. The instant I fell dead,
a thousand sails refilled. That shore ahead
was windswept, too. My wind. A maiden tongue
made mute too soon revealed itself in red
dust syllables across your endless young
heroic sacrifices. Ten years flung
away to sate ambition — yet my voice
remained through every moment's respite wrung
from stormworn nights. And now your fatal choice
of bedmate hears the future in my cry:
this cold black wind that blows you home to die.

Gone 11 Days Before Anyone Could Be Bothered to Look in White Cloud, Michigan by Michael Harrington

For Amanda Lankey

Long before
my skin sloughed
away,
my mouth filled with
leaves
and loam,
and earthworms nested
in the broken bowl
of my skull—

you

had already pinned
the tattered letter
to my chest.

You—

(all of you)

picked up your rod,
stepped into the boat,
the proud prow slicing
the perfect, silent,
still glass
of morning—
it made all the difference.

Eugenics in the Modern Era by Colleen Anderson

doctors take the women, the poor
and immigrants; the darker the better
pin them and muffle their screams—

the missing restrained, spread for exams
with forceps, glinting scalpels, they prime
the specimens for new incubations

they puncture, dissect, scoop out all
they determine makes a woman rebel
ovaries, breasts, vulvic extremities

they probe, rearrange, insert terrible designs—
pollens, insect larvae, mycelial cells
each set to produce prescribed desires

docile, decorative, obsequious beings
those who survive, first of their kind
holotypes encased in prisons of glass

plump, pulsing, convulsing women
turn, twist, call out and claw

erupting rashes, boils, eyes bleeding tears

spitting, they shriek, vomit pale strands
spin glistening cocoons, chrysalides
a tomb's quiet in a snowfall of spores

three days—a stillness—then soft gnawing
sends a message, from each cage, a creature
wriggles forth, stands naked, and shivers

they stare with unreadable obsidian prisms
as powdery wings unfold from their backs
unrepentant, they cough a colorful melange

the plume obscures, then blooms into moths
aloft, and butterflies flutter through air vents
escaping, a hurricane dispersing, infesting

experimenters succumb, miasma-infused
lepidopteran women reformed, evolving
resilient imagoes fly free

*Over 60,000 women were sterilized
in US state-run eugenics programs through the 20th century

Not That Kind of Compost by Viggy Parr Hampton

Every spring, my neighbors
Marvel at my azaleas.
Vivid red, violent magenta, scarlet with a bleeding edge
Burst from my yard like hands punching through grave dirt.
Every fall, my neighbors
Marvel again at my azaleas,
But this time
They're scratching their heads,
Asking me, asking themselves,

"How do you make azaleas bloom in the fall?"
"What kind of fertilizer keeps them so alive?"

I smile, showing my pointed teeth,
Look down at my fertile earth bashfully.
I remind them dead things make the best potions for
Eternal life,
And I let them think I mean compost—
Rotten banana peels, coffee grounds, withered vegetables.

I don't mean compost.
I smile again, mouth closed,

Using the toe of my boot to push the soil
Back over Mother's bony finger.

Boneless by Graham Masterton

It has no swirling robes, no slicked-back hair
No glittering eyes to fill your heart with dread.
Although your house is silent you won't hear it there
When it comes creeping in to share your bed.

It has no bones at all, except for teeth
It's flat and grey and slippery like a sheet
Your front door may be locked but it can slide beneath
And climb your stairs with rubbery hands and feet.

It wakes its sleeping victims when it flops on top.
It smothers them and then it starts to bite.
It drains their blood, and leaves them not a single drop
So that they end up stiff, and plaster-white.

It comes in winter long before the springtime thaws.
Bezkost, it's called in Poland – Boneless here
The Poles place draught excluders under doors
Not to save energy, but from fear.

Pine Box by Paul Lonardo

Approach her with fear
Grandma asleep in coffin
Lips glued speak no more

Pretty Little Thing by Julia Jackson

A weak little thing with brittle bones.
A pretty little thing you leave at home.
A bruised little thing with a throat of violet blooms.
A quiet little thing motionless below you.

Your emerald eyes went wide like saucers,
A moment of disbelief.
This pathetic girl could never do such a thing.
This damaged girl could never hurt a fly.

This angry girl grinning above you,
Her hand steady with a knife.

I only wish it had lasted longer.
Your sputtering and agonizing pain.
Your last few breaths of panic.
Your tongue coated in a metallic taste.

I'll play the moment in my memory,
Will honor you in this way.
My lips will wear a smile,
Match the ear-to-ear shape I traced.
Remember the way the blade felt,
Within the soft of your neck.

How easily your skin tore apart,
Your hands clawing to put everything back.

You never saw me coming,
Your trophy should have been on her shelf.
But doesn't that make this so much sweeter?
My love, aren't you so impressed?

Rest easy now, not a soul will know.
I'll echo your words and play my role.
I'm just some pretty little thing.

This Is What We Do to Gender Inspectors, So Don't Get Any Ideas by Stacie Herrington

They thought I was a trans girl.
I told them they were wrong.
But when they asked
then what are you?
I couldn't answer.

All I could say was I liked to run,
so I joined the track team.
Before the legislation.
Now I was up for inspection.
They thought I was a trans girl.

The room was so vinyl, so fluorescent,
disinfected, medicinal—as if
healing were on the table.
The men put on gloves.
What did they expect to touch?
A woman had to be there to witness.
It's protocol, and don't think too hard about why.
She smiled. Just another shift.

I said you should leave.
She said I'm here to be a friend. And, it's a policy.
I said I don't want to hurt you.
And the men said it was time for them to see.
Gender should not be left unknown.

What if it's unknowable? I said.
But I couldn't stop them from looking.

One gouged out his own eyes with a speculum.
The other fell to his knees, began praying in tongues.

The woman was already out the door.
Her screams tore the fabric of spacetime.

I put my uniform back on.
I ran back to practice.
   I like to run.

No one asks anymore.
Go on, though. Ask me what I am.
Stare into the gendervoid.

Ennui by Jean-Marie Romana

Walled-up ghost
waiting for the world to end.

The Bile Tooth by Stephanie M. Wytovich

Inspired by the Hydnellum peckii fungus

You lick weeping skin:
my body, a mansion of rot
against arachnid eyes,
the blood juice of spores.

I taste of expired cream,
the jaundice of fruit. You bleed
the teeth of devils, lay down
warts between my toes,
eyes capped, lips devoured
my body the house
   you've decided to haunt.

I Write a Rite of Pyrite by Katherine Quevedo

He insults me, so
I perform the rite
I'd sworn never,
never to commit
to the page, ever,

and all his digits
limn the mineral
he becomes, and
his shape morphs
to cuboid-crystal,

mental into metal
head, right angles
and splicing ache
with flatness and
firmness all over,

scared of all this
becoming, of all
this new self and
loss of old, of the

layers spreading

from his outside
in, and his voice
freezes halfway
through a shriek,
and my screams

endure, because
I have witnessed
an inelegant end
and wish I could
undo it *but can't*.

I Will Come For You by Paul Duff

Forest dark hides your face.
Your boot against my skull,
Playful kicking, testing.
I struggle to roll away,
My body manages only a profound exhale.

A chuckle, deep and long.

"Welcome back," your voice an unwanted touch.
"You can't really move right now,
Sorry, not sorry."
That chuckle again, followed by a cough.

You take my wedding ring,
My good luck necklace,
My watch, and wallet, and phone.
You take my connections to the world.
I will trace back, I will come for you.

You roll me face down,
Press my face into moist decay.
My mind chants nonsense,
"Ashes to ashes, dust to dust,
Ashes to dust, dust to ashes."

You begin a leisure stomping
Of my feet, of my ankles.
You pleasure in the cracking
Of my legs, and knees, and hips.
Hands, wrists, arms, elbows, shoulders.

You take a breather, chuckle,
Cough, spit, and chuckle some more.
My ribs splinter from a few swift kicks.
You roll the mass, the mess, of my body

To face the sky, to breathe the night.

"Say Goodnight," you tease, and then jump.
My skull gives way under your boots.
I will come for you.
First, I must rest.
First, I must rot.

The Bundles by Annie Neugebauer

Moving stillness,
inside the car in the early hours,
a tank of silence within the ordinary roar of an engine,
held calm through the neighborhood
looking out at dark, silent dark,
and then a figure.

She is so unexpected there,
crossing the street with a bundle on her chest,
that my mind first tries to make her backwards,
a backpack on her front, or a burden carried too high,
but she walks right across my headlights—brake—and,
no, yes, it is definitely a baby.

The silence in my car's shell pounds.

She does not slow, or speed, or cringe, or wave,
and then there are more figures and bundles
and they glide from between shadows
as if on conveyer belts,
as if their feet should not show beneath long robes,
but they wear pajamas and sweatpants and sneakers,

and they walk now, entranced,

all to one unseen end.

I hear something, roll down my window.
A baby cries.

My two babies, at home in bed. Surely.
I creep forward, edge the car between passers.
That person holds a larger child.
That person drags one along by the hand.

But my kids are safe. Home with my partner.
Safe, safe. Safe, I chant, driving faster and faster,
and I wish so hard I begin to believe it,
until I turn down our street
and recognize a figure
holding two familiar bundles.

Above us all, the moon hangs suspended
as if at the end of a noose.

Night Stalker by Pauline Yates

You thought I didn't know that you were stalking me,
An easy victim, clueless to their plight,
Another kill would carve your name in history,
My scream would sate your sinful appetite.

An easy victim, clueless to their plight,
A blade, your choice of weapon for the killing spree,
My scream would sate your sinful appetite,
I'll deny your lust for blood, though it excites me.

A blade, your choice of weapon for the killing spree,
You seek infamy, like vampires crave the night,
I'll deny your lust for blood, though it excites me,
You should see your shocked expression when I bite.

You seek infamy, like vampires crave the night,
Another kill would carve your name in history,
You should see your shocked expression when I bite,
You thought I didn't know that you were stalking me.

Playthings by Melissa Burkley

We are born in a box, plastic prison, cardboard cage, jackaled squeals of delight, greedy hands rip paper, crack cellophane, wrench us from the womb, peanut-butter-sticky fingers rake our mint-condition skin, painted lips, cornsilk hair, love us so hard it hurts.

Stop! Treat us gently, touch us softly—pleas trapped behind sealed smiles, rough hands strip us naked, clothe us, strip us, twist our head, pose our arms, spread our legs, malevolent puppeteer, our bodies are not our own, our bodies are not our own, our bodies are their playthings.

Foot cram too tight shoe, bite off a toe—spit—to make it fit, tongues, slick with ice cream, slide across our synthetic skin, pausing at lavish bosom, slender thigh, hourglass waist, but the sand is running out, our beauty has an expiration date.

A little older, a little wiser, realization a tightening vice, these things with giant hands, rictus grins, are ancient deities, we, their mere creations, mass produced for pleasure, accept this—devoted disciples, we aim to please—but these gods demand the impossible: to sexualize us, to strip us of our sexuality.

Malformed feet perched high on plastic pedestals, so narrow, so precarious, we are guaranteed to fall, they tell us our only purpose is to attract Mr. Right, when we do, we are shamed, they tell us our only worth is in creating life, when we do, we are abandoned, discontinued, it happened to Midge—it will happen to us all.

Make them happy—it is what we were made for, so we are told—a Sisyphean task that keeps our heads swiveling, but we try, we walk on tippy toes, swivel our hips, bend our molded backs until our polymer vertebrae splinter from pressure, our reward, exiled to the bottom of the toy bin.

Time passes—paint fades, hair mats, porcelain skin turns dingy, no longer enamored with our beauty, they invent new uses for our bodies, scissors to hair, flame to skin, safety pins driven through soft palms, a virgin sacrifice, if we are lucky, they bury us in a shallow grave and forget about us, many are not that fortunate.

Donna: he gifted his doll with a dreamhouse, then a broken nose, cracked ribs, a bubble bath of boiling hot water—skin splits, spits, curls back in revulsion as eyes melt into blue smears.

Kelly: a makeover with pruning shears, snip of an ear, a nose, excavated eyes as blood rouges pale cheeks, her broken body laid to rest in a claw-footed coffin.

The unnamed girl from Hong Kong: four of them took turns, like well-mannered children do, punching, kicking, biting, violating, then recess is over, time to clean up, flesh boiled in pots, bones tossed in the trash, head stuffed in the hollows of an old Hello Kitty doll.

This is how they love us, love so hard it hurts, break us apart, limb from limb, snap us back together, break us apart, back together, again.

                        And again.
                        And again.

Three Final Girls Take the Border Bridge (Orient, Maine) by Patricia Flaherty Pagan

Country roads take us home, sleep stories in our ears
lasso truth in Wonder Woman bathing suits
in the way-back, our pillows hide contraband oranges
Veronica and two Bettys from our comics, finally
three final girls cross the border bridge
to warm rocks, cool waters, twirling silver
explode red fireworks for independence

trip, trap, trip, trap, trip, trap, went the bridge

frog-hunt with old pots through swamp grass
algae lurks, throw us in learn to swim, leeches
cling to our troll-beast climbing from his lair
white, wide eyes stare and sear
rapier nose cuts our cheeks
ravenous as a mountain lion stalking,
we smell campfires and Jiffy Pop

trip the trap, trip the trap, dynamite the bridge

We burn his bridge, this memory thief
thumb-crush soft troll eyeballs

THREE FINAL GIRLS TAKE THE BORDER BRIDGE (ORIENT, MAINE) BY...

speedboat wakes chuckle and dance, defiant
we listen as the lake beckons
three final girls finally strike
snatch back our August joys
keeping them safe on sun-warmed innertubes
Swim across, swim across, defy customs.

Transit Zombies by Jamal Hodge

The shrieking centipede of wheels
roars sparks,
spitting out walking bones.

We offer our flesh,
sitting on warmed tongues,
in the acidic gut of miserable faces,
ear to ear, eyes in all directions.

The very soul feels crowded,
the nostrils full,
ears hear, none listen.

By the time we get to where we're going,
we're no longer ourselves,
eviscerated in toxic juices,
from a million invasive moods.

Six sets of 54-inch-wide mouths slide open,
regurgitating our exit,
a joyless mass of walking bones,
ready to zombie the day.

Lone Star Blues by Robert Perez

In this desolate place all her dreams
died. She followed in her father's footsteps
to the same small town slaughterhouse.
There was no escaping this pastoral purgatory
where the crows know everyone's secrets,
lost in an endless maze of corn.

When he first witnessed her in action
he was captivated by awe and fear

of her dead eye kills. Lovestruck by her
brutal swing of the butcher's mallet.
Her large hands helped place Texas
BBQ on the world's map, claiming
more lives than Old Sparky.

After months of gathering courage
he approached as she unleashed
her hair from its gore spackled netting
and it went wild like a murder
of crows calling out his deepest desire.
His invitation to the only diner
for miles dangled like a carcass
hooked and flayed under the buzzing

florescent lights. She took a small bite
out of her ham and mustard on white,
covering her mouth as she chewed,
before politely declining and offering
vague honesty, "My husband…is hungry."

At the end of the day she returns
home to feed her bedbound beloved,
whose bedsores weep against the walls
of the room which he can no longer leave.

At the end of the night she returns
to the processing line for her shift
where every skull-shattering blow to the brain
comes with a whisper of her husband's name.

immersion learning by Carlie St. George

the parallels are well-documented, final girls and fairy tale girls, but still, we should do something. we should start a cultural exchange program. the things we could teach one another; for example, resurrection: have you found your sisters in bloody pieces and reassembled all the wet chunks? did your brother become a bird (temporarily) when you gathered and buried all his bones? if a horse loses its head, can it even offer you advice? we can teach you such magics; in turn, please instruct us on the art of the machete. please teach us that particular flavor of terror: lemonade infused with adrenaline. jiffy pop and certain death. we can be clever, and we can be beautiful, but rarely are we primal. strip us bloody and raw and desperate. wolves will swallow us. we'll bite our way out.

Menopause Monsters by Louise Worthington

She plants terrible clockwork in my skull,
Tick-tick-tick, bombs behind each ear.
Mirrors show my face falling
as wax beneath flame, features sliding
From moorings.
I walk through rooms like a ghost.

She pulls each fibre past endurance, measuring
How far before breaking.
Skin, once taut drum of youth,
Slackens as sails in windless seas.
Drapes in surrender,
Banners after defeat.

With surgical tools she unpicks memory's lock,
Emptying drawers of names, certainties,
Pilfering patience from my treasury.
She, pyromaniac, strikes matches against bones.
My blood ignites, a spontaneous combustion.
I burn like Joan at unseen stakes.

Her hands, deft as pickpocket's, search me.

But this: she cannot steal what forms
In the crucible of her torture.
Iron, hammered white-hot, emerges stronger.
Beneath scalded skin, a new self calcifies,
A terrible goddess born from theft and flame.

Raft Bodies by Erik Hofstatter

I wore this dead girl on my back like a parachute.
Jumped from the bridge, pulled on her short arms.
Hoping she would open.
That something would fly out of her mouth.
Corpse words I knew.
But she said nothing.
Silent hearts bully the water. It's theirs now.
We tie parent bodies together, fun little rafts.
And paddle in pursuit of her.

The Water Horse by Manny Blacksher

His Lordship, pissed, painless, crooning "She Moved
Through the Fair," put a shoe in each shuck
in the moon field when he halted to look
at a mare. The shine off her flanks proved
those clefts between stars were only as dark
as the rest of her. Black, unhaltered
no man's filly, unless his luck faltered
He swung up and kicked towards Cromleach Park

whereat she flung fifty furlongs and plunged
in a bog his agent recorded as "fen
in the northwest hectare" but countrymen
named Brown Widow's Lap. That baronet sponged
some more pints before she would quarter
him, hooves sharp as knackers' knives, broach
his neck like a magnum decanted for loach
savor the malts in the ruby red porter

It's Not a Game to the Dead by Juleigh Howard-Hobson

First, the candles will go out, one by one.
the air will grow cold, the room will turn black
for a second, while low whispering's spun
across the darkness. Don't pull your hands back
now, unless you don't want to complete what
you've started. Beware: if it's not finished
it will never end. See it through, see that
you close what's opened. People shouldn't wish
to play games with the dead, but since you did
there's nothing to do but feel the planchette
whirl around the board in circles. Don't kid
yourself, you're playing with a real spirit
there. Spell out goodbye before it can find
a way to stay here. The dead are not kind.

Odessa Black by David Ghilardi

Putin's war crushed me
Shattered remnants of my limbs
Clumps of muck sticking
To oozing stumps bubbling red
Like ripe Kiev grapes in Spring.

(Odessa Black is an actual vintage in Ukraine)

The Ghoulish Abyss by Sara Tantlinger

I am the sunless depth
nothing more than a sighing
susurrus, swimming through saline
and hiding half-buried in sediment

Hungry, I search the ocean's floor,
mouth a swirling void sucking
fish skin into my maw, crunching
snails against needle-sharp teeth

Slick and sleek, I glow
in bioluminescent victory—
my lure flashing purple-blue
hues to attract new prey

Humans follow in steel machines,
as they always do, unable to resist
exploring where they aren't wanted,
but if I am to be named sea devil

Then let their flesh find me
in the sullen brine where I evolve,
growing larger despite icy settings,
forever a strange beast, resplendent

In light and horror, fangs eager
to pull fresh, meaty meals onto
my mouth's spiked floor; cunning
and ghoulish, I am the last denizen

Of the darkest deep, the patient
angler greeting tender bodies,
welcoming carcasses into eternal
abyss, a final seawater shroud.

Glass Alphabet by Ivy Grimes

Acquire glass asps and adders in aquariums.
Buy brie and blood to bake in glass.
Cry glass curtains for cold coverings
and dig deep in death's dust with glass dewclaws.
Even a glass elephant eats existential eggs
far from the fodder of faded glass foals; free from
gloom, glass gods glow with gesture.
Heaven hates harvests of glass hands.
Ice isn't iambic glass, isn't ill ivory—
just as glass jaws jut, jeweled with jealousy.
Kidneys kissed by glass keys, kilted kin
leave glass lemons in the lawn's labyrinth.
Make me miles of glass miasma, mourned by mice,
not nutrients for neutral nouns, not nameless nadirs.
Ovens oblige, obey the opulence of glass oaks
plying the porous perennials with glass pollen.
Quit questioning the quiet and quit the glass queens
reaching for glass rulers on ribbon rugs,
searching for sport south of glass sickness.
Turn to thieves, the thunder of glass thorns thumping
under udders, unglassed ugliness, unusual as us
vying veiled with visitors, vital as volcanic glass vineyards
where water's white walls wind through glass wives.
X-ray this xylitol Xanadu for glass exes,

yet yon glass yard yawns, yields yesterday
zesting glass zones with zeniths of zen.

Fruit Fly Summer by Jamie Lackey Stefko

A fruit fly floats
in the milk she only left
for a second.

A black speck, still
struggling,
in a sea of white.

The milk was almost
sour anyway, edging
toward foulness, toward coagulation
toward rot.

She dumps it down the sink
disturbing the fly's extensive family, who
swarm up as a buzzing wave.

She has killed hundreds of them,
maybe thousands, with traps
with sticky paper, with vinegar
and sugar and dish soap, but they
are endless.

She should have

drank the milk anyway.
She is thin
and weak
and tired.

Her lips, her toes, her fingertips
tingle, almost stinging.
The first dreaded sign.

She doesn't want to die,
doesn't want to leave her kitchen
to the fruit flies.

She can only prevent one.
She lights a candle
turns on the gas
and walks away.

The fruit flies settle
behind her.

What a Mother and Daughter Know about Breathing by Crystal N. Ramos

My mother tried to
reassure me when I
unwrapped her genetic
present of non-epileptic
seizures.

"Don't worry," she said.
"If you pass out,
your body will start
to breathe again."

Words with the same taste as
when she said the doctor's
shot wouldn't hurt.

Today, I couldn't
reach my phone to call
for help before my limbs
started twitching and my lungs
froze.

Black is crowding my

eyes.

The Planet's Darkside by Deborah L. Davitt

In your ears, the hiss of compressed air
as darkness presses against your eyes

there's no air that you can breathe
outside your helmet
no sunlight on this side of the planet;
there should be no life

and yet there is,
all dark-adapted eyes and teeth,
sensing the pressure of your footfalls
on the cold earth beneath

you can feel them approaching
but not see them,
and you spin, raising a spar of metal
scavenged from your crashed ship

—there's already blood on it—

and in the lights of your helmet
you catch sight of one gaping maw

as it plunges towards you
you stab upwards

—feel the shock of impact, the strain against your arms—

and another body goes limp against you
and you recoil in horror
as its exoskeleton scrapes down the front
of your suit, tearing at controls and valves

Inhale. Exhale. Trust in the suit
to keep you alive, Plod to the east,
heading for the terminator,
where light and life live
on this tide-locked planet—

feel the eyes still on you,
sense the rush of movement,
spin, turn, slash—

there's more of them than there are of you
and miles to go before you sleep.

Summer's Gone by Azzurra Nox

It was the summer of everlasting fire
Your kisses like coals burned right through me.
Your charm too thick to see past its golden veneer.
Just nineteen and I was on my knees, desperate for your love
But I never could've imagined the macabre dance you had in mind
When you pulled me into the Nebrodi.
My mouth was thick with apologies, spilling blood upon your feet
But your knife was filled with rage, and I was now your pin cushion
Your blade came down forty-seven times to the beat of the cicadas' August song.
The sky bled with your lies as I stared up, my fingers desperately clutching at the life slipping violently away from me.
This cannot be the end…
This cannot be….but it is and no amount of tears will chase Hades from me.
Your words echoed in the dark – *I will never leave you.*
But here I am in the dark alone.
Were there signs? I was taught that love must hurt
And I let it leave bitemarks on my skin, I let it yank my curls and shatter me.
You learn to love cruelty when it's dressed in gold.
Are they going to blame me for his mistake? *She was asking for it.*
That autumn, dead violets bloomed in my lungs and by winter the maggots had feasted on my stomach, had made a buffet out of my eyes.
Then everything went silent –
When spring cracked the sky with thunder and Zeus's bolts revived me

I traced my steps back to you.
Remember when you said I was too young, too weak?
But now, look who's on their knees, begging
My protector, *my killer*
I embrace you until your bones crack
The sweetest symphony is your funeral dirge
And now that I lay us down to sleep
Lips pressed against yours –
Your blood pours into my mouth and all I can feel is
Alive.

Flesh Tears by Daniel Kipps

Flesh tears in the dark
Bones snap as it drags her near
Eyes watch, hollow, cold.

Peonies by Eric Machan Howd

> "On a day like today, it's worth saying,
> I believe survivors. Men must not close
> our eyes and minds to what happens
> to women in this world."- Neil Gaiman

I learned how they open from a master who asked me
to clench my hand into a fist and hold it in front of him.
He made his fingers into tiny ants and slowly marched
toward my tightly wound hand - smiling as he crept
closer to me - knowing what would happen - beaming

from the expectation of seeing me see it for the first time.
And when the ants reached my palm they slowly began
peeling fingers away from the center - layer upon layer
rooting for the dreams I held so safe and tight inside
until what was once a fist was now an open flower.
Smooth curved petals reflecting sunlight and summer
a Morpheus of ants busily gathering over me to take
what they can before dusk calls my fist back again.

Portrait of a Slaughterhouse by Grace R. Reynolds

Acrid red splatters white aprons,
freezer burn encrusts on bone

Cadavers gutted, pelvis to sternum,
dangling while fluorescent lights hum

Mesh gloves turn metal, grinding flesh churns,
meat saw melodies

A hook in the spine, watchful dead eyes,
gaping jaws and cut out tongues

Jailhouse freezer, dense clouds of vapor,
asphyxiation wrapped in plastic

Inhalation—
Internal conflagration—
Realization—

No one to hear you scream.

Night Shift at the Asylum by Spencer Keene

His throat-shredding shriek
reaches me from the end of
the unlit hall,
a violent call to
jacket-bound arms or
a desperate plea for release.

I imagine him there,
drowning in infernal echoes,
confined to his
cushioned chamber,
strapped and
heavy-dosed.

A flicker of sympathy

takes me by surprise
as I rise and go forth,
inhaling insane mists
as I march
the black tunnel.

Delighted by the thud
of skull-on-door
I pace the polished floor,
cradle the key
in my clammy palm
and slip it gently home.

A stare into a pair of
coal-black hollows,
a mangled mouth,
a split forehead and
torn tangles of
blood-tattered hair.

He screams at me
in my voice.

The Memory of Her Demise by Richard Groller

Fool that I was, I thought I could
find my way, lost in these woods.
I searched for a path to somewhere or when,
found a cabin by a stream in a hidden glen.
As the twilight waned, I did not see
the skeleton outside, that should have warned me.
As I stepped on the threshold I became transfixed,
as I witnessed the horror of the Nix.
St. Elmo's fire traced the room,
unfolding a scene of imminent doom
young mother with four children under three
put her babes to sleep, then offered a plea
that her husband could please return to her soon,
a prayer to God by the light of the moon.
As she lay down she was startled awake,
with a feeling of dread she could not mistake.
She lit a candle to brighten the gloom,
in the flickering light, the floor moved in the room.
Then pincers and talons embraced from behind,
fangs opened her neck, and fear filled her mind.
As thousands of spiders flowed cross the floor,
the bodies of children now covered in gore.

Her dread gave her voice "Not the children!" she cried,
then she heard a short laugh, "A wish before you die?"
All that she said was "Remember me, and mine."
And so here I now stand, transfixed, for all time,
reliving the memory of her demise.

me, mary and todd by Jan-Andrew Henderson

She said, "My name is Mary and this is my son, Todd
We like to spread the word of God
By selling jokes from door to door
It's a bit new age, but all the rage."
They asked if I would like a ride.
I said "Yes, please and tell me more"
Unhooked my pack and climbed inside

They offered me a rubber nun
A CD of the Rolling Stones
Just a harmless bit of fun.
But I think saintly teeth and bones
Sell better than this blasphemous junk
So most of Mary, I converted
While the road was still deserted
And bits of Todd are in the trunk

For our sins I made them pay
They bought from me eternal peace
And moving in a mysterious way
I keep ahead of the police.
Carrying the good Lord's crosses

I make my profit from his losses

Wandering lonely as a cloud
That's Todd's face on the Turin Shroud

Sleep ("haamujen uni") by Ron Riekki

When things are at their worst, I can't sleep.
When things are at their best, I can't sleep.
I can sleep when things are in the middle. Otherwise,
I wake in the middle of the night. I shower. It's how I kick in
my parasympathetic nervous system. The problem is
I can shower five times a night. You know how there'll
sometimes be a Starbucks right across the street from another Starbucks.
Well, I can take a shower right after I've taken a shower. It can be every other
hour.
I think of the war. At its worst, we didn't have time to shower, to drink, to
piss.
Especially at night. Things always seemed worse at night. We did more
bombings then. We created more ghosts then. We'd create ghosts, filling
the night with instant ghosts. The V.A., I've found, is great
if you have killed one person; if you pointed a gun at someone
and ghosted them, the enemy 'them,' then the V.A. has empathy,
sympathy. Whatever the word is. But what if you helped
kill thousands and thousands of people? I think of the word 'helped.'
Help! They only come at night, the dead. They only come at night,
often. They surround my bed, my mattress coffin, the night's hunger,
anger . . . hangry. The night's hunger, sad . . . had. I'm not friends
with them. I lie there, paralyzed. I find if I shower, hydrate,
and piss, the ghosts visit less, but the other trigger is the night.
If I could just stop the night, I would be perfectly fine. I'd be

perfect. I've been psychoanalyzed to death. The psychiatrist's
couch-coffin. He tries to have me bring the dead in the room.
I've only done it once, awakening from my wakefulness with him
hovering over me, others too, staff, yelling for me that I'm safe,
but never yell at someone that they are safe, don't scream You are safe!
with your eyes lit up like demons. Never do that. Allow me to
demonstrate what the night looks like when the blizzards of my mind
strike. I was told by my father that if you look deep into a blizzard
you will see all of the dead from your hometown struggling to wave
to you, furiously, for you to see them, right on the edge, of the blankness
of white, that in many ways, looks like an empty page, like what is buried
below this line. Stare into it, the space below. Can you see the dead waving?

Necromantic by Christine N. Rifkin

I love this woman lying on the ground next to me
But things are never easy.

There's the way my life turned out and the way it should have been
And they lie on the opposite poles of the Earth.

My father, torn to pieces by a mechanical demon, left me a lonely child
His soul trapped forever, never there to let me leech the comfort from it.

I should have listened to my uncle, who tried to pull the bile hidden within my veins
But that metallic word called "love" stings my throat as I speak.

I lie next to her, the clumped mix of blood and hair jutting from her scalp
I prayed she'd look at me, provide me with the love my father could never give.

But things were never easy
I blame myself, clutching her close despite the coldness of her skin.

Can you still love me?
Can you still feel me?

Her body doesn't move, and neither does mine

I loved this woman lying on the ground next to me.

The Wasp in the Wine by Vishesh Abeyratne

They sink their mandibles
into grapes' flesh,
corroding it with bitter yeast,
readying the gore within
to be liquefied for our pleasure

Is it any wonder, then,
when the glass is drained,
that the barbs propelled
from your reptilian tongue
carry stings of such venom

that they sink embedded
as silk-white eggs
into the tissue of the object
of your bile

abiding, waiting,
hatching, crawling
parallel to veins,
shuffling the skin

Mother, dear mother,

it whines in her skull,

I have grown strong jaws,
let me eat my way out

I have grown thick wings,
let me fly

I have grown a syringe
filled with toxins,
let me inject them
into his flesh

Let me be lethal

The Drowning of the Virgin Queen by Andrew Robertson

'Immortal', she whispered. 'I was to be immortal'
Her hair, red and wet, stained the pillow
Deep and red like his blood that was denied her
And her own which now also betrayed, and sat in corrupted pools inside her

He knew of her. He found her. He showed her his teeth in Paris
Near blue in the moonlight reflecting off the river
Sharp and long, closing on the obscene, sending shocks along the invisible seam
Separating what they each were, this divide inspiring a fascination in both

As the cold water whispered along the bank, night stretched into a flowing eternity
Stitched in waves to many more dark nights, and so many words that became tales
Of desire, destruction, terrible beauty and ruthless ambition, his dark path and her own
Born and bound in a time so long ago when everything seemed possible
And they were so close to that timeless want being satisfied

They had a twin obsession that behaved as a foolish child, ambivalent to stormy endings

They were fecund, a reservoir of manic desires between them
Each to create in their own way, with a desire to combine these twin streams
To one day feel these roar and course through one vein, powerful, devastating, beautiful…

And then the sun rose and the dewy underside of hope turned dry
The dark dream vanished into the unwelcome newness of a bird's song
If it was ever more than a feverish hope born in a catacomb

Absence lay before her like an arid, forlorn land

Eyes closed, she felt the weight of his denial as it pulled her down
Into the bed, wet and corrupted with her suffering, confusion, still unfinished
Each memory was a pocket full of bones longing to be back underground
Time like water rippled over the inky unknown which lay ahead of her

She told his stories
Her words made endless worlds for him, shared his wicked beauty
But like that first night, he never came back, never fulfilled that riverside promise to her

Time like water rippled, pulled up and around her by the relentless Moon of mortality
Until it's another day, and the water is still
And her own story ends
While his night remains endless

Author Bios

R. J. Joseph is an award winning, Shirley Jackson and Stoker Award™ nominated Texas based writer/speaker/editor. Her creative and academic work examines the intersections of race, gender, and class in the horror genre and popular culture. R.J. is an instructor at The Speculative Fiction Academy and a co-host of the Genre Blackademic podcast. She has most recently been at work with Raw Dog Screaming Press on their new novella line, Selected Papers from the Consortium for the Study of Anomalous Phenomena. She occasionally peeks out on various social media platforms from behind @rjacksonjoseph or at www.rhondajacksonjoseph.com.

Greg Jones is a horror poet and artist whose first collection entitled "Meet Me In the Flames" was published by WildInk publishing in October 2024. A follow up collection coming October of 2026 will be entitled "Apologies To the Morning" and will see him pushing boundaries further into bleak and forbidden territory. Hard at work on a collection of short stories, as well, he resides in the suburbs of Milwaukee with his wife, three daughters and an ever growing collection of skin covered tomes.

K.A. Schultz writes with pictures and draws with words. An art historian, bilingual (German) 1st generation American, Kimann is a fan of all things darkly romantic – and romantically dark. She is the author of the horror short story and poetry collections NEITHERIUM, GÖTHIQUE, and KHRYSTMASS; and of JACOB A Denouement in One Act, as well as A LETTER FROM KRAMPUS.

Angela Sylvaine is a Bram Stoker Award nominated author and self-proclaimed cheerful goth who writes speculative fiction and poetry. Details about her sci-fi horror comedy novel, Frost Bite, her slasher novella, Chopping Spree, and her short story collection, The Dead Spot: Stories of Lost Girls, as well as her dozens of short fiction and poetry publications can be found at angelasylvaine.com.

Cassondra Windwalker earned a BA of Letters from the University of Oklahoma. Born and raised on the red clay, she's wandered the sticky corn fields of the Midwest, the frozen seas of the Wild North, and frequently rests her wings where orange skies meet purple mountains. She's the author of nine novels and three collections of poetry and does her best to keep fed a menagerie of stray critters, cryptids, marooned kelpies, and lost specters.

Tiffany Michelle Brown is a Los Angeles-based writer who once had a conversation with a ghost *over a pumpkin beer. She is the author of How Lovely To Be a Woman: Stories and Poems and co-host of the Horror in the Margins podcast. Her stories and poetry have been featured in publications by Cursed Morsels Press, Ominous Thrill, Tenebrous Press, Black Spot Books, Death Knell Press, and the NoSleep Podcast. To learn more about her work, visit www.tmbwrites.com.*

Daniela E. is an Italian writer. Since she learned to read and write at the age of five, books have become an integral part of her life. Passionate about the occult and paranormal and a lover of splatter, she decides to dedicate her writing to thrillers and horror. Graduated in Literature and specialized in Modern Linguistics, since 2023 she has been recognized as a member of the Horror Writers Association and in 2024 she joined the Crime Writers' Association. A self-published writer, Daniela has published five books: the noir Loren, the horror Kohu (also available in English) the splatter thriller series The Terry Brooke Series, La Giostra dei Clown (also available in English under the name The Clowns' Carousel) and La Giostra delle bambole di pezza and in 2025 published the collection of horror stories Buonanotte e sogni d'oro. Very active in supporting self publishing and self authors, she believes that literature should be free and not controlled and shackled by companies and entrepreneurs. Daniela currently lives in her hometown with her dog Argon. Web site: www.danielae.com

AUTHOR BIOS

Born and raised in New York's haunted Hudson Valley and more recently a resident of North Carolina's equally haunted Cape Fear region, **JG Faherty** *is the author of 25 books, 3 short story collections, 1 poetry collection, and more than 95 short stories. He's been a finalist for both the Bram Stoker Award (twice) and ITW Thriller Award, and his poetry and short stories have appeared in numerous print and online markets. He writes adult and YA horror, science fiction, dark fantasy, and paranormal romance, his works ranging from quiet, suspenseful horror to action-packed paranormal thrillers. He is proud to be a relative of Mary Shelley. You can follow him on X, Facebook, and Instagram as @jgfaherty.*

Author, editor, entertainment journalist and illustrator **Gabrielle Faust** *is best known for her internationally renowned post-apocalyptic cyberpunk vampire series ETERNAL VIGILANCE. To date she has successfully released thirteen novels and anthologies in the horror, cyberpunk, paranormal thriller and poetry genres. Her work has appeared in magazines and websites such as Weird Tales Magazine, SciFi Wire, Girls and Corpses Magazine, Austin Food and Wine Magazine, Fatally Yours, Examiner, Doorways Magazine, Fear Zone, and Gothic Beauty Magazine, as well as various anthologies. In addition, she has served as the lead editor on seven novels and two anthologies, including Blood Games: A Vampire Anthology. She is represented by the renowned New York literary agency The Knight Agency. In 2013 she was crowned "Vampire Royalty of New Orleans". Faust is currently at work on several new literary projects, as well as her first cookbook. When she is not writing Faust is an avid painter and singer-songwriter. More information about Gabrielle Faust can be found on her website gabriellefaust.com.*

Caitlin Marceau *(she/they) is a queer Canadian author and illustrator known for her award-winning novella This Is Where We Talk Things Out. Their forthcoming work includes their novella's sequel, All Roads Lead Us Home, as well as their fourth collection, Loose Ends. When she's not busy writing, she's focused on her work with Hedone Books (hedonebooks.com), a queer, neurodivergent, and femme-owned Canadian publishing house. For more, find them on social media or check out CaitlinMarceau.ca.*

Ann K. Schwader *lives and writes in Colorado. Her newest collection,* Unquiet Stars, *is out now from Weird House Press. Two of her earlier collections,* Wild Hunt of the Stars *(Sam's Dot, 2010) and* Dark Energies *(P'rea Press, 2015) were Bram Stoker Award Finalists. She was the SFPA's 2018 choice for Grand Master, and is a two-time Rhysling Award winner.*

Michael Aaron Harrington *is a poet and scribbler that lives along the Front Range of Northern Colorado. He enjoys hanging out his two French Bulldogs, Boxer-mix, reading scary books and poetry, and playing boardgames with his family. He's just foolish enough to agree to run his first marathon over fifty.*

Multiple award-nominated and award-winning author ***Colleen Anderson*** *has been widely published across seven countries, with works appearing in publications such as* Weird Tales, Cemetery Dance, *and* Amazing. *Her Rhysling Award-winning poem "Machine (r)Evolution" is featured in Tenebrous Press's* Brave New Weird, *and she is a two-time winner of the SFPA's dwarf poetry contest. Colleen is the author of several poetry collections, including* The Lore of Inscrutable Dreams, I Dreamed a World, *and* Weird Worlds. *Raw Dog Screaming Press has just published her fourth poetry book,* Vellum Leaves and Lettered Skins.

Viggy Parr Hampton*, MPH is an epidemiologist, content marketing strategist, host of the podcast "Horror Humor Hunger," and the author of* A Cold Night for Alligators, Much Too Vulgar, *and* The Rotting Room. *She is a graduate of Georgetown University and Emory University's Rollins School of Public Health. She is also a member of the DreadPop Magazine team, producing the popular YouTube segment "Tag Team Tales of Terror," where she challenges fellow horror authors to create a progressive story with her.*

Graham Masterton *is mainly recognized for his horror novels but he has also been a prolific writer of thrillers, disaster novels and historical epics, as well as one of the world's most influential series of sex instruction books. He became a newspaper reporter at the age of 17 and was appointed editor of Penthouse magazine at only 24. His first horror novel* The Manitou *was filmed with Tony Curtis playing* the lead, and three of his short horror stories were filmed by Tony Scott for The Hunger TV series. Ten years ago Graham turned his hand to crime novels and White Bones, set in Ireland, was a Kindle phenomenon, selling over 100,000 copies in a month. This has been followed by eleven more bestselling crime novels featuring Detective Superintendent Katie Maguire, the latest of which is Pay Back The Devil. In 2019 Graham was given a Lifetime Achievement Award by the Horror Writers Association. His horror novel Szpital Filomeny was voted best horror novel of 2023 by the readers of Lubimy Czytac. The Prix Graham Masterton for the best horror fiction in French has been awarded annually for the past twelve years, and nine years ago he established an annual award for short stories written by inmates in Polish prisons, Nagroda Grahama Mastertona 'W Więzieniu Pisane.' He is currently working on new horror and crime novels. He is also co-authoring a collection of short stories based on Slavic mythology with the Polish psychiatrist and writer, Karolina Mogielska. Their jointly-written stories have already appeared in Phantasmagoria magazine, and in anthologies published in Poland, Obiata and Nocne Mary as well as in the form of chapbooks in Poland, Greece and the Czech Republic. Graham has completed a new horror novel in the series featuring Det Sgt Jamila Patel and Det Jerry Pardoe, House of Flies.

Paul Lonardo is a freelance writer, poet, and author with numerous titles, both fiction and nonfiction books. Paul has placed short stories and nonfiction pieces in various genre magazines and ezines. He is a contributing writer for several publications, including Tales from the Moonlit Path, and an HWA member.

Julia Jackson is the author of Powder & Poison, is featured in various international horror anthologies, and is a member of the Horror Writers Association. After a near-fatal car accident, Julia turned to writing as part of recovery and now crafts chilling stories that strip away the masks women wear, revealing emotional depth and damage. Julia has had more surgeries than Frankenstein, is a creature of the night like Batman, and creates memorable heroes and monsters of her own. Julia teaches mindful writing at Kristin Dwyer's Breaking the Story Retreat, as well as to the online writing community. When Julia is not writing, she works in Corporate Communications and watches an unhealthy amount of ghost hunting shows and horror movies. Connect with her on Instagram @juliajacksonauthor or visit juliajacksonauthor.com

Stacie Herrington writes horror and reviews horror movies. Her latest short stories appear in Roadkill: Texas Horror by Texas Writers Vol. 10 (Hellbound Books) and The Writing on the Wall: a Horror Tribute to Iron Maiden (Wicked Ouija Press). Other recent work appears in the Horror Writers Association Poetry Showcase XI, StokerCon 2025 Souvenir Anthology, and the Black Hare Press Patreon. Stacie reviews horror movies for Last Girls' Club and on The Podcast Compels You. Follow @herringtonstacie on Instagram for publishing updates.

Jean-Marie Romana is an accursed poet from California.

Stephanie M. Wytovich is an American poet, novelist, and essayist. She is a recipient of the Bram Stoker Award, the Elizabeth Matchett Stover Memorial Award, the 2021 Ladies of Horror Fiction Writers Grant, and the Rocky Wood Memorial Scholarship for non-fiction writing. Follow Wytovich at https://www.stephaniemwytovich.com/ and on Twitter and Instagram @SWytovich and @thehauntedbookshelf. You can also sign up for her newsletter at https://stephaniemwytovich.substack.com/.

Katherine Quevedo was born and raised near Portland, Oregon, where she works as an analyst and lives with her husband and two sons. She is the author of the Elgin Award-winning chapbook The Inca Weaver's Tales (Sword & Kettle Press, 2024) and the fantasy novella Thrice Petrified (Of Metal and Magic Publishing, 2025). Her poetry has been nominated for the Pushcart Prize and Rhysling Award and appears in Asimov's, Old Moon Quarterly, Extrasensory Overload, Coffin Bell, HWA Poetry Showcase Vol. XI, and elsewhere. When she isn't writing, she enjoys watching movies, playing old-school video games, singing, belly dancing, and making spreadsheets. Find her at www.katherinequevedo.com.

Paul Duff is a lifelong reader and writer. Owned by cats. Healed by gardens. Obsessed by the dark. Can be found on the socials as @lifewithtomcat.

AUTHOR BIOS

Annie Neugebauer is a novelist, blogger, nationally award-winning poet, and two-time Bram Stoker Award-nominated short story author. She's the author of the novella trilogy The Outsiders Sequence (The Extra, The Other, and The Spare) as well as her debut collection You Have to Let Them Bleed. You can visit her at AnnieNeugebauer.com.

Pauline Yates is an award-winning Australian author of horror, science fiction, and poetry. A BookFest, Aurealis, and Australasian Shadows Awards winner, her work spans novels, novellas, short fiction, and poetry, often exploring themes of memory, identity, and the uncanny. Visit her website at https://paulineyates.com/ or find her on socials @midnightmuser1.

Melissa Burkley has a Ph.D. in Psychology and is a renowned expert on sexism and racism. Her literary work has appeared in Tainted Love: Women in Horror Anthology, Night Terrors (Vol. 8 & 14), Women in Horror Annual 2, Hinnom Magazine, Gamut Magazine and Poets & Writers Magazine. Her poetry has appeared in Spooky Magazine and the HWA Poetry Showcase XI. Visit www.melissaburkley.com

Patricia Flaherty Pagan lives in a brown house near the sea with her family. She is the award-winning author of "Trail Ways Pilgrims" and "Enduring Spirit: Stories." Her poetry has been published in anthologies and journals, including "Moras Vitae," "Blood and Bourbon," "Nightmare Melodies," and "Horror Writers Association Poetry Showcase VIII."

Jamal Hodge is a Bram Stoker Award & Elgin Award finalist and a multi-award-winning filmmaker. His work explores the interplay between darkness and redemption. Hodge's debut, The Dark Between the Twilight, placed 3rd in the full-length book category of the 2025 Elgin Awards, while his poem "Colony" placed second in the 2022 DwarfStars. He has also been nominated for 3 Rhysling awards. Jamal served as editor of the debut anthology Bestiary of Blood: Modern Fables & Dark Tales, which made the BSFA long-list. in 2024. His latest project, Everything Endless (2025), is a collaborative poetry collection with SFPA Grand Master Linda

D. Addison that merges cosmic law with call-and-response revelations.

Robert Perez sleeps at the bottom of the ocean. Urban legend whispers that the writer can be summoned into your dreams if you read his work to a jack-o-lantern. You can find his poems and stories in the Horror Writers Association Poetry Showcase Volumes II, III, IV (Special Mention), V, X, and XI (Featured Poet), Five Minutes at Hotel Stormcove, Community of Magic Pens, Greater Than His Nature, Cursed Cooking, and more. Robert Perez recently graduated and works as a psychological counselor providing therapy. Follow @RobertPerez.bsky.social to keep up with future projects.

Carlie St. George is a speculative writer, Shirley Jackson Award finalist, and British Fantasy Award finalist from Northern California. Her poetry can be found in Uncanny and PANK, and her short fiction can be found in several anthologies and magazines, such as PseudoPod, The Dark, and The Best American Science Fiction and Fantasy. Her debut collection YOU FED US TO THE ROSES is available from Robot Dinosaur Press. Find her on Bluesky, Instagram, or on her blog My Geek Blasphemy, where she mostly talks about TV, writing, and her adorable monster cats.

Louise Worthington is a UK-based author and poet. She is a Pushcart nominee and her Gothic novel Rosie Shadow has been praised as "chilling and addictive". She writes horror, dark psychological suspense and literary fiction. Her poetry and short fiction have appeared in journals such as Eye to the Telescope, Orbis, Coffin Bell and 34 Orchard. She can be found at https://https://louiseworthington.com/

Erik Hofstatter is a dark fiction writer, born in the wild lands of the Czech Republic. He roamed Europe before subsequently settling on English shores, studying creative writing at the London School of Journalism. He now dwells in Kent, where he can be encountered consuming copious amounts of mead and tyrannizing local peasantry. His work appeared in various magazines and podcasts around the world such as Morpheus Tales, The Literary Hatchet, Wicked Library, Manor House Show, and The Black Room Manuscripts Volume IV. Other works include The Hurricane

AUTHOR BIOS

Caged Inside of Her and Stone Martyrs.

Manny Blacksher is an author and editor living in Birmingham, AL. His poems have appeared in magazines, journals, and anthologies that include the HWA Poetry Showcase, Space and Time, The Maynard, Unsplendid, Belfast's Fortnight, and Poetry Ireland Review. Three of his poems will appear in Triggerfish Critical Review's July 2025 Issue.

Juleigh Howard-Hobson's dark speculative poetry has appeared in The Dead Lands, Midnight Echo, The Audient Void, Dreams and Nightmares, Under Her Skin (Black Spot), Vastarien: Women's Horror (Grimscribe), and many other places. Nominations include the Pushcart, Elgin, Best of the Net and Rhysling. Her latest book is Curses, Black Spells and Hexes (Alien Buddha). An active member of both the SFPA and the HWA, she lives in a suitably haunted house on the edge of the known world.

David Ghilardi is the author of the Dark Chicago series. Please see Davidghilardi.com for more. All 11 of his books are available on Amazon.

Sara Tantlinger is the author of the Bram Stoker Award-winning The Devil's Dreamland: Poetry Inspired by H.H. Holmes, and the Stoker-nominated works To Be Devoured and Cradleland of Parasites. She has also edited Not All Monsters and Chromophobia. She is an active HWA member and also participates in the HWA Pittsburgh Chapter. She embraces all things macabre and can be found at saratantlinger.com and on Instagram @inkychaotics

Ivy Grimes lives in Georgia and has work published in places like The Baffler, The Magazine of Fantasy & Science Fiction, ergot., Cosmic Horror Monthly, and Vastarien. Her collection Glass Stories is available from Grimscribe Press, and her debut novel The Ghosts of Blaubart Mansion from Cemetery Gates. Please visit her at www.ivyivyivyivy.com.

Jamie Lackey lives in Pittsburgh with her husband and their cats. She has had over

200 short stories published in places like Beneath Ceaseless Skies, Apex Magazine, and Escape Pod. She has a novella and two short story collections available from Air and Nothingness Press, and she's created six successful crowdfunding campaigns to self-publish a novel, two novellas, a novelette, and three short story collections. In addition to writing, she spends her time reading, playing tabletop RPGs, baking, mushroom hunting, and hiking. You can find her online at www.jamielackey.com.

Crystal N. Ramos *lives with her husband and two children in Georgia, USA. She has won the Maggie Award for Excellence in Prepublished Romantic Fiction twice and has an MA in Professional Writing from Kennesaw State University. Some of her shorter work has appeared in Black Hare Press: Year Six, Stygian Lepus: Issue 5, and The Dr. T. J. Eckleburg Review. In her imaginary spare time, she likes to knit, cross-stitch, and play Minecraft.*

Deborah L. Davitt was raised in Nevada, but currently lives in Houston, Texas with her husband and son. Her award-winning poetry and prose have appeared in over seventy journals, including F&SF, Asimov's, Analog, and Lightspeed. For more about her work, including her Elgin-placing poetry collections, Bounded by Eternity and From Voyages Unreturning, see www.deborahldavitt.com.

Azzurra Nox is a Pushcart Prize nominee and Killer Shorts Winner. She was born in Catania, Sicily and has led a nomadic life since birth. Her current works are I Want Candy, Girl That You Fear, and Into the Dread Unkown: Women in Horror Anthology. She currently resides in So-Cal. You can find her online at https://theinkblotters.com or Instagram @divazura.

Based on England's south coast, **Daniel Kipps**, previously a game industry veteran (16 years as a game designer and director), lives with his family and pet dog. He's enjoyed a successful career in game design, but his passion for writing horror stories has led him to become a full-time author. Daniel enjoys creating slow burn, Lovecraftian inspired stories, which build dread and make the reader feel uneasy before finishing with a large, action-filled, horrific climax.

Eric Machan Howd's sixth collection of poetry, "Universal Monsters," was published by The Orchard Street Press in 2021. He is currently working on an H.P. Lovecraft erasure project and two other poetry collections on his fear of flowers and his world travel. His poetry has been published in many magazines, journals, and anthologies across the world.

Grace R. Reynolds is an American speculative fiction writer. She was raised in New Jersey and graduated from Rutgers University with a BA in Political Science, Labor Studies, and a minor in the Russian language. Having lived in seven states, she currently calls Maryland 'home,' where she writes dark fiction inspired by her heritage, eastern European history and folklore, the Gothic, as well as horrific and dystopian settings. In addition to her short fiction, she is the author of Lady of the House and two other collections of poetry. These include The Lies We Weave, which was nominated for the SFPA Elgin Awards, and Midnight Blue. Her debut novella, Neon Moon, will appear in the Spring of 2026 through Dark Matter Ink.

Spencer Keene (he/him) is a lawyer and writer from Vancouver, BC. His short fiction and poetry have appeared in a variety of print and digital publications, including SAD Magazine, Sea to Sky Review, Candlelit Chronicles, and Star*Line Magazine. Find more of Spencer's work at www.spencerkeene.ca.

Richard Groller is an author of fiction and non-fiction. His non-fiction book credits include co-author of The Warrior's Edge (with Janet Morris and COL John Alexander)and Chief Researcher and contributing author to The American Warrior (Janet and Chris Morris, Eds.). A member of HWA and SFPA, Rich is a contributor to the Heroes in Hell series, and has to date been published in 7 volumes of the shared universe anthology by Baen Books and Perseid Press. He is published in 4 volumes of the Sha'Daa: Tales of the Apocalypse series (created by Michael H. Hanson and published by Moondream Press). He has been published by Iron Clad Press in 2 volumes of John Manning's Night Chills horror anthologies: Terror by Gaslight and Dark Corners and by Perseid Press in John Manning's horror anthology What Scares the Boogeyman?. He has been published in the Horror Writers Association Poetry Showcase, Volumes III and IV, and is Editor of the The Book of Night, an illustrated book of macabre poetry, also published by Moondream Press. His latest works are in Not to Yield (3 Raven's Publishing) and Standing Against All Fears (Last Brigade Universe).

Jan-Andrew Henderson (J.A. Henderson) is the author of 40 children's, teen, YA and adult fiction and non-fiction books - published in the UK, USA, Australia, Canada and Europe by Oxford University Press, Collins, Hardcourt Press, Amberley Books, Oetinger Publishing, Mainstream Books, Black and White Publishers, Mlada Fontana, Black Hart, Three Ravens and Floris Books. He has been shortlisted for sixteen literary prizes in the UK and Australia and is the winner of the Doncaster Book Prize, The Aurealis Award and the Royal Mail Award - Britain's biggest children's book prize.

Ron Riekki has been awarded a 2014 Michigan Notable Book, 2015 The Best Small Fictions, 2016 Shenandoah Fiction Prize, 2016 IPPY Award, 2019 Red Rock Film Fest Award, 2019 Best of the Net finalist, 2019 Très Court International Film Festival Audience Award and Grand Prix, 2020 Dracula Film Festival Vladutz Trophy, 2020 Rhysling Anthology inclusion, and 2022 Pushcart Prize. Right now, Riekki's listening to SKRZ w/ atmos.vera (Věra Riekki Koss) on Prague's NTS radio.

Christine N. Rifkin is a Florida-based horror author and screenwriter whose short stories have appeared in the Black Hare Press anthology Eerie Christmas 3 and the Creepy Podcast. Her short script "Right Hand Man" was the winner of Best Short Screenplay at the 2023 Freak Show Film Festival and her first horror novella, Reverie, was released by Baynam Books Press in the Fall of 2025. When she isn't writing, Christine spends most of her time on adventures with her husband, Scott, or at home lounging with their two cats, Covie and Dr. Victoria Frankenstein. You can see more of her work at christinenrifkin.com.

Vishesh Abeyratne is a playwright and poet based in Ottawa, Ontario, Canada. He currently works as Literary Manager for Teesri Duniya Theatre and was playwright-in-residence at the Great Canadian Theatre Company. His poems have been published in Bywords.ca, Flo Literary Magazine, and Montreal Serai (forthcoming in April 2025). Plays include *Exposure (published by YouthPLAYS), Blood Offering, White Lion, Brown Tiger,* and *The Agony Market.*

Andrew Robertson is a queer horror writer. He recently launched his debut solo short story collection, InhuMANities, dark fiction focussed on the role men play in making the world a more horrific place. He also shares Dearly Departed, a dual-author short story collection, with Sèphera Girón.

Andrew has three short stories in the Lunar Codex: #WritersOnTheMoon. These stories are part of the largest single collection of contemporary art ever put on the Moon.

A lifelong fan of horror, Andrew's work has appeared in multiple anthologies and literary magazines. He is the founder of The Great Lakes Horror Company small press and podcast and is a member of the Horror Writer's Association.

Find him on Instagram @andrewawesome76 and BlueSky @andrewawesome.bsky.social.

www.ingramcontent.com/pod-product-compliance
Lightning Source LLC
Chambersburg PA
CBHW071307040426
42444CB00009B/1915